Martha's Lady

Sarah Orne Jewett

MARTHA'S LADY.

I.

ONE day, many years ago, the old Judge
Pyne house wore an unwonted look of gayety and youthfulness. The high-fenced
green garden was bright with June flowers.
Under the elms in the large shady front
yard you might see some chairs placed near
together, as they often used to be when the
family were all at home and life was going
on gayly with eager talk and pleasure-mak-
ing; when the elder judge, the grandfather,
used to quote that great author, Dr. Johnson,
and say to his girls, " Be brisk, be splendid,
and be public."

One of the chairs had a crimson silk
shawl thrown carelessly over its straight back,
and a passer-by, who looked in through the
latticed gate between the tall gate-posts with
their white urns, might think that this piece
of shining East Indian color was a huge red
lily that had suddenly bloomed against the
syringa bush. There were certain windows

thrown wide open that were usually shut,
and their curtains were blowing free in the
light wind of a summer afternoon; it looked
as if a large household had returned to the
old house to fill the prim best rooms and find
them full of cheer.

It was evident to every one in town that
Miss Harriet Pyne, to use the village phrase,
had company. She was the last of her family, and was by no means old; but being the
last, and wonted to live with people much
older than herself, she had formed all the
habits of a serious elderly person. Ladies
of her age, something past thirty, often wore
discreet caps in those days, especially if they
were married, but being single, Miss Harriet clung to youth in this respect, making
the one concession of keeping her waving
chestnut hair as smooth and stiffly arranged
as possible. She had been the dutiful com-
panion of her father and mother in their
latest years, all her elder brothers and sisters
having married and gone, or died and gone,
out of the old house. Now that she was left
alone it seemed quite the best thing frankly
to accept the fact of age, and to turn more
resolutely than ever to the companionship of
duty and serious books. She was more seri-

ous and given to routine than her elders
themselves, as sometimes happened when the
daughters of New England gentlefolks were
brought up wholly in the society of their
elders. At thirty-five she had more reluc-
tance than her mother to face an unfore-
seen occasion, certainly more than her grand-
mother, who had preserved some cheerful
inheritance of gayety and worldliness from
colonial times.

There was something about the look of
the crimson silk shawl in the front yard to
make one suspect that the sober customs of
the best house in a quiet New England village were all being set at defiance, and once
when the mistress of the house came to stand
in her own doorway, she wore the pleased but
somewhat apprehensive look of a guest. In
these days New England life held the neces-
sity of much dignity and discretion of behavior; there was the truest hospitality and good
cheer in all occasional festivities, but it was
sometimes a self-conscious hospitality, followed by an inexorable return to asceticism
both of diet and of behavior. Miss Harriet Pyne belonged to the very dullest days
of New England, those which perhaps held
the most priggishness for the learned pro-

fessions, the most limited interpretation of
the word "evangelical," and the pettiest indifference to large things. The outbreak of
a desire for larger religious freedom caused
at first a most determined reaction toward
formalism, especially in small and quiet vil-
lages like Ashford, intently busy with their
own concerns. It was high time for a little
leaven to begin its work, in this moment
when the great impulses of the war for lib-
erty had died away and those of the coming
war for patriotism and a new freedom had
hardly yet begun.

The dull interior, the changed life of the
old house, whose former activities seemed to
have fallen sound asleep, really typified these
larger conditions, and a little leaven had
made its easily recognized appearance in the
shape of a light-hearted girl. She was Miss
Harriet's young Boston cousin, Helena Vernon, who, half-amused and half-impatient
at the unnecessary sober-mindedness of her
hostess and of Ashford in general, had set
herself to the difficult task of gayety. Cousin
Harriet looked on at a succession of ingen-
ious and, on the whole, innocent attempts at
pleasure, as she might have looked on at the

frolics of a kitten who easily substitutes a
ball of yarn for the uncertainties of a bird
or a wind-blown leaf, and who may at any
moment ravel the fringe of a sacred curtain-
tassel in preference to either.

Helena, with her mischievous appealing
eyes, with her enchanting old songs and her
guitar, seemed the more delightful and even
reasonable because she was so kind to every-
body, and because she was a beauty. She
had the gift of most charming manners.
There was all the unconscious lovely ease
and grace that had come with the good breed-
ing of her city home, where many pleasant
people came and went ; she had no fear, one
had almost said no respect, of the individual,
and she did not need to think of herself.
Cousin Harriet turned cold with apprehension when she saw the minister coming in at
the front gate, and wondered in agony if
Martha were properly attired to go to the
door, and would by any chance hear the
knocker ; it was Helena who, delighted to
have anything happen, ran to the door to
welcome the Reverend Mr. Crofton as if he
were a congenial friend of her own age.
She could behave with more or less propriety
during the stately first visit, and even con-

trive to lighten it with modest mirth, and to extort the confession that the guest had a tenor voice, though sadly out of practice ; but when the minister departed a little flattered, and hoping that he had not expressed himself too strongly for a pastor upon the poems of Emerson, and feeling the unusual stir of gallantry in his proper heart, it was Helena who caught the honored hat of the late Judge Pyne from its last resting-place in the hall, and holding it securely in both hands, mimicked the minister's self-conscious entrance. She copied his pompous and anxious expression in the dim parlor in 'such delicious fashion that Miss Harriet, who could not always extinguish a ready spark of the original sin of humor, laughed aloud.

"My dear!" she exclaimed severely the next moment, "I am ashamed of your being so disrespectful!" and then laughed again, and took the affecting old hat and carried it back to its place.

"I would not have had any one else see you for the world," she said sorrowfully as she returned, feeling quite self-possessed again, to the parlor doorway; but Helena still sat in the minister's chair, with her small feet placed as his stiff boots had been, and a copy of his solemn expression before they came to speaking of Emerson and of the guitar. "I wish I had asked him if he would be so kind as to climb the cherry-tree," said Helena, unbending a little at the discovery that her cousin would consent to laugh no more. "There are all those ripe cherries on the top branches. I can climb as high as he, but I can't reach far enough from the last branch that will bear me. The minister is so long and thin" —

"I don't know what Mr. Crofton would have thought of you; he is a very serious young man," said cousin Harriet, still ashamed of her laughter. "Martha will get the cherries for you, or one of the men. I should not like to have Mr. Crofton think you were frivolous, a young lady of your opportunities" — but Helena had escaped through the hall and out at the garden door at the mention of Martha's name. Miss Harriet Pyne sighed anxiously, and then smiled, in spite of her deep convictions, as she shut the blinds and tried to make the house look solemn again.

The front door might be shut, but the garden door at the other end of the broad hall was wide open upon the large sunshiny garden, where the last of the red and white peonies and the golden lilies, and the first of the tall blue larkspurs lent their colors in generous fashion. The straight box borders were all in fresh and shining green of their new leaves, and there was a fragrance of the old garden's inmost life and soul blowing from the honeysuckle blossoms on a long trellis. It was now late in the afternoon, and the sun was low behind great apple-trees at the garden's end, which threw their shadows over the short turf of the bleaching-green. The cherry-trees stood at one side in full sunshine, and Miss Harriet, who presently came to the garden steps to watch like a hen at the water's edge, saw her cousin's pretty figure in its white dress of India muslin hurrying across the grass. She was accompanied by the tall, ungainly shape of Martha the new maid, who, dull and indifferent to every one else, showed a surprising willingness and allegiance to the young guest.

"Martha ought to be in the dining-room, already, slow as she is; it wants but half an hour of tea-time," said Miss Harriet, as she turned and went into the shaded house. It was Martha's duty to wait at table, and there had been many trying scenes

and defeated efforts toward her education.
Martha was certainly very clumsy, and she
seemed the clumsier because she had replaced
her aunt, a most skillful person, who had
but lately married a thriving farm and its
prosperous owner. It must be confessed
that Miss Harriet was a most bewildering
instructor, and that her pupil's brain was
easily confused and prone to blunders.
The coming of Helena had been somewhat
dreaded by reason of this incompetent service, but the guest took no notice of frowns
or futile gestures at the first tea-table, except to establish friendly relations with
Martha on her own account by a reassuring
smile. They were about the same age, and
next morning, before cousin Harriet came
down, Helena showed by a word and a
quick touch the right way to do something
that had gone wrong and been impossible to
understand the night before. A moment
later the anxious mistress came in without
suspicion, but Martha's eyes were as affectionate as a dog's, and there was a new look
of hopefulness on her face; this dreaded
guest was a friend after all, and not a foe
come from proud Boston to confound her
ignorance and patient efforts.

The two young creatures, mistress and maid, were hurrying across the bleaching-green.

"I can't reach the ripest cherries," explained Helena politely, "and I think that Miss Pyne ought to send some to the minister. He has just made us a call. Why Martha, you have n't been crying again!"

"Yes 'm," said Martha sadly. "Miss Pyne always loves to send something to the minister," she acknowledged with interest, as if she did not wish to be asked to explain these latest tears.

"We 'll arrange some of the best cherries in a pretty dish. I 'll show you how, and you shall carry them over to the parsonage after tea," said Helena cheerfully, and Martha accepted the embassy with pleasure. Life was beginning to hold moments of something like delight in the last few days.

"You 'll spoil your pretty dress, Miss Helena," Martha gave shy warning, and Miss Helena stood back and held up her skirts with unusual care while the country girl, in her heavy blue checked gingham, began to climb the cherry-tree like a boy.

Down came the scarlet fruit like bright rain into the green grass.

" Break some nice twigs with the cherries and leaves together ; oh, you 're a duck, Martha ! " and Martha, flushed with delight, and looking far more like a thin and solemn blue heron, came rustling down to earth again, and gathered the spoils into her clean apron.

That night at tea, during her hand-maiden's temporary absence, Miss Harriet announced, as if by way of apology, that she thought Martha was beginning to under-stand something about her work. " Her aunt was a treasure, she never had to be told anything twice ; but Martha has been as clumsy as a calf," said the precise mistress of the house. " I have been afraid some-times that I never could teach her anything. I was quite ashamed to have you come just now, and find me so unprepared to entertain a visitor."

" Oh, Martha will learn fast enough be-cause she cares so much," said the visitor eagerly. " I think she is a dear good girl. I do hope that she will never go away. I think she does things better every day, cou-sin Harriet," added Helena pleadingly, with all her kind young heart. The china-closet door was open a little way, and Martha heard every word. From that moment, she not only knew what love was like, but she knew love's dear ambitions. To have come from a stony hill-farm and a bare small wooden house, was like a cave-dweller's coming to make a permanent home in an art museum, such had seemed the elaborateness and elegance of Miss Pyne's fashion of life; and Martha's simple brain was slow enough in its processes and recognitions. But with this sympathetic ally and defender, this exquisite Miss Helena who believed in her, all difficulties appeared to vanish.

Later that evening, no longer homesick or hopeless, Martha returned from her polite errand to the minister, and stood with a sort of triumph before the two ladies, who were sitting in the front doorway, as if they were waiting for visitors, Helena still in her white muslin and red ribbons, and Miss Harriet in a thin black silk. Being happily self-forgetful in the greatness of the moment, Martha's manners were perfect, and she looked for once almost pretty and quite as young as she was.

"The minister came to the door himself, and returned his thanks. He said that cherries were always his favorite fruit, and he was much obliged to both Miss Pyne and Miss Vernon. He kept me waiting a few minutes, while he got this book ready to send to you, Miss Helena."

" What are you saying, Martha? I have sent him nothing!" exclaimed Miss Pyne, much astonished. " What does she mean, Helena?"

" Only a few cherries," explained Helena. " I thought Mr. Crofton would like them after his afternoon of parish calls. Martha and I arranged them before tea, and I sent them with our compliments."

" Oh, I am very glad you did," said Miss Harriet, wondering, but much relieved. " I was afraid " —

" No, it was none of my mischief," answered Helena daringly. " I did not think that Martha would be ready to go so soon. I should have shown you how pretty they looked among their green leaves. We put them in one of your best white dishes with the openwork edge. Martha shall show you to-morrow; mamma always likes to have them so." Helena's fingers were busy with the hard knot of a parcel.

" See this, cousin Harriet!" she announced proudly, as Martha disappeared round the corner of the house, beaming with the pleasures of adventure and success. "Look! the minister has sent me a book: Sermons on *what?* Sermons — it is so dark that I can't quite see."

"It must be his 'Sermons on the Seriousness of Life;' they are the only ones he has printed, I believe," said Miss Harriet, with much pleasure. "They are considered very fine discourses. He pays you a great compliment, my dear. I feared that he noticed your girlish levity."

"I behaved beautifully while he stayed," insisted Helena. "Ministers are only men," but she blushed with pleasure. It was certainly something to receive a book from its author, and such a tribute made her of more value to the whole reverent household. The minister was not only a man, but a bachelor, and Helena was at the age that best loves conquest; it was at any rate comfortable to be reinstated in cousin Harriet's good graces.

"Do ask the kind gentleman to tea! He needs a little cheering up," begged the siren in India muslin, as she laid the shiny black volume of sermons on the stone doorstep with an air of approval, but as if they had quite finished their mission.

" Perhaps I shall, if Martha improves as much as she has within the last day or two," Miss Harriet promised hopefully. " It is something I always dread a little when I am all alone, but I think Mr. Crofton likes to come. He converses so elegantly."

II.

These were the days of long visits, before affectionate friends thought it quite worth while to take a hundred miles' journey merely to dine or to pass a night in one another's houses. Helena lingered through the pleasant weeks of early summer, and departed unwillingly at last to join her family at the White Hills, where they had gone, like other households of high social station, to pass the month of August out of town. The happy-hearted young guest left many lamenting friends behind her, and promised each that she would come back again next year. She left the minister a rejected lover, as well as the preceptor of the academy, but with their pride un-wounded, and it may have been with wider outlooks upon the world and a less narrow sympathy both for their own work in life and

for their neighbors' work and hindrances.
Even Miss Harriet Pyne herself had lost
some of the unnecessary provincialism and
prejudice which had begun to harden a
naturally good and open mind and affectionate heart. She was conscious of feeling
younger and more free, and not so lonely.
Nobody had ever been so gay, so fascinat-
ing, or so kind as Helena, so full of social
resource, so simple and undemanding in her
friendliness. The light of her young life
cast no shadow on either young or old com-
panions, her pretty clothes never seemed to
make other girls look dull or out of fashion.
When she went away up the street in Miss
Harriet's carriage to take the slow train
toward Boston and the gayeties of the new
Profile House, where her mother waited im-
patiently with a group of Southern friends,
it seemed as if there would never be any
more picnics or parties in Ashford, and as if
society had nothing left to do but to grow
old and get ready for winter.

Martha came into Miss Helena's bed-
room that last morning, and it was easy to
see that she had been crying; she looked
just as she did in that first sad week of

homesickness and despair. All for love's sake she had been learning to do many things, and to do them exactly right; her eyes had grown quick to see the smallest chance for personal service. Nobody could be more humble and devoted; she looked years older than Helena, and wore already a touching air of caretaking.

"You spoil me, you dear Martha!" said Helena from the bed. "I don't know what they will say at home, I am so spoiled."

Martha went on opening the blinds to let in the brightness of the summer morning, but she did not speak.

"You are getting on splendidly, are n't you?" continued the little mistress. "You have tried so hard that you make me ashamed of myself. At first you crammed all the flowers together, and now you make them look beautiful. Last night cousin Harriet was so pleased when the table was so charming, and I told her that you did everything yourself, every bit. Won't you keep the flowers fresh and pretty in the house until I come back? It's so much pleasanter for Miss Pyne, and you 'll feed my little sparrows, won't you? They 're growing so tame."

"Oh, yes, Miss Helena!" and Martha looked almost angry for a moment, then she burst into tears and covered her face with her apron. "I couldn't understand a single thing when I first came. I never had been anywhere to see anything, and Miss Pyne frightened me when she talked. It was you made me think I could ever learn. I wanted to keep the place, 'count of mother and the little boys; we 're dreadful hard pushed. Hepsy has been good in the kitchen; she said she ought to have patience with me, for she was awkward herself when she first came."

Helena laughed; she looked so pretty under the tasseled white curtains.

"I dare say Hepsy tells the truth," she said. "I wish you had told me about your mother. When I come again, some day we 'll drive up country, as you call it, to see her. Martha! I wish you would think of me sometimes after I go away. Won't you promise?" and the bright young face suddenly grew grave. "I have hard times myself; I don't always learn things that I ought to learn, I don't always put things straight. I wish you would n't forget me ever, and would just believe in me. I think it does help more than anything."

"I won't forget," said Martha slowly. "I shall think of you every day." She spoke almost with indifference, as if she had been asked to dust a room, but she turned aside quickly and pulled the little mat under the hot water jug quite out of its former straightness; then she hastened away down the long white entry, weeping as she went.

III.

To lose out of sight the friend whom one has loved and lived to please is to lose joy out of life. But if love is true, there comes presently a higher joy of pleasing the ideal, that is to say, the perfect friend. The same old happiness is lifted to a higher level. As for Martha, the girl who stayed behind in Ashford, nobody's life could seem duller to those who could not understand; she was slow of step, and her eyes were almost always downcast as if intent upon incessant toil; but they startled you when she looked up, with their shining light. She was capable of the happiness of holding fast to a great sentiment, the ineffable satisfaction of trying to please one whom she truly loved. She never thought of trying to make other people pleased with herself; all she lived for was to do the best she could for others, and to conform to an ideal, which grew at last to be like a saint's vision, a heavenly figure painted upon the sky.

On Sunday afternoons in summer, Martha sat by the window of her chamber, a low-storied little room, which looked into the side yard and the great branches of an elm-tree. She never sat in the old wooden rocking-chair except on Sundays like this; it belonged to the day of rest and to happy meditation. She wore her plain black dress and a clean white apron, and held in her lap a little wooden box, with a brass ring on top for a handle. She was past sixty years of age and looked even older, but there was the same look on her face that it had sometimes worn in girlhood. She was the same Martha; her hands were old-looking and work-worn, but her face still shone. It seemed like yesterday that Helena Vernon had gone away, and it was more than forty years.

War and peace had brought their changes and great anxieties, the face of the earth was furrowed by floods and fire, the faces of mistress and maid were furrowed by smiles and tears, and in the sky the stars shone on as if nothing had happened. The village of Ashford added a few pages to its unexciting history, the minister preached, the people listened ; now and then a funeral crept along the street, and now and then the bright face of a little child rose above the horizon of a family pew. Miss Harriet Pyne lived on in the large white house, which gained more and more distinction because it suffered no changes, save successive repaintings and a new railing about its stately roof. Miss Harriet herself had moved far beyond the uncertainties of an anxious youth. She had long ago made all her decisions, and settled all necessary questions; her scheme of life was as faultless as the miniature landscape of a Japanese garden, and as easily kept in order. The only important change she would ever be capable of making was the final change to another and a better world; and for that nature itself would gently provide, and her own innocent life.

Hardly any great social event had ruffled the easy current of life since Helena Vernon's marriage. To this Miss Pyne had gone, stately in appearance and carrying gifts of some old family silver which bore the Vernon crest, but not without some protest in her heart against the uncertainties of married life. Helena was so equal to a happy independence and even to the assistance of other lives grown strangely dependent upon her quick sympathies and instinctive decisions, that it was hard to let her sink her personality in the affairs of another. Yet a brilliant English match was not without its attractions to an old-fashioned gentlewoman like Miss Pyne, and Helena herself was amazingly happy; one day there had come a letter to Ashford, in which her very heart seemed to beat with love and self-forgetfulness, to tell cousin Harriet of such new happiness and high hope. "Tell Martha all that I say about my dear Jack," wrote the eager girl; "please show my letter to Martha, and tell her that I shall come home next summer and bring the handsomest and best man in the world to Ashford. I have told him all about the dear house and the dear garden; there never was such a lad to reach for cherries with his six-foot-two." Miss Pyne, wondering a little, gave the letter to Martha, who took it deliberately and as if she wondered

too, and went away to read it slowly by
herself. Martha cried over it, and felt a
strange sense of loss and pain ; it hurt her
heart a little to read about the cherry-pick-
ing. Her idol seemed to be less her own
since she had become the idol of a stranger.
She never had taken such a letter in her
hands before, but love at last prevailed,
since Miss Helena was happy, and she
kissed the last page where her name was
written, feeling overbold, and laid the envel-
ope on Miss Pyne's secretary without a
word.

The most generous love cannot but long
for reassurance, and Martha had the joy of
being remembered. She was not forgotten
when the day of the wedding drew near,
but she never knew that Miss Helena had
asked if cousin Harriet would not bring
Martha to town ; she should like to have
Martha there to see her married. "She
would help about the flowers," wrote the
happy girl; "I know she will like to come,
and I 'll ask mamma to plan to have some
one take her all about Boston and make her
have a pleasant time after the hurry of the
great day is over."

Cousin Harriet thought it was very kind

and exactly like Helena, but Martha would
be out of her element; it was most im-
prudent and girlish to have thought of such
a thing.   Helena's mother would be far
from wishing for any unnecessary guest just
then, in the busiest part of her household,
and it was best not to speak of the invita-
tion.   Some day Martha should go to Boston if she did well, but not now.   Helena
did not forget to ask if Martha had come,
and was astonished by the indifference of
the answer.   It was the first thing which
reminded her that she was not a fairy
princess having everything her own way in
that last day before the wedding.   She
knew that Martha would have loved to be
near, for she could not help understanding
in that moment of her own happiness the
love that was hidden in another heart.
Next day this happy young princess, the
bride, cut a piece of a great cake and put
it into a pretty box that had held one of her
wedding presents.   With eager voices call-
ing her, and all her friends about her, and
her mother's face growing more and more
wistful at the thought of parting, she still
lingered and ran to take one or two trifles
from her dressing-table, a little mirror and

some tiny scissors that Martha would remember, and one of the pretty handker-
chiefs marked with her maiden name.
These she put in the box too; it was half
a girlish freak and fancy, but she could
not help trying to share her happiness, and
Martha's life was so plain and dull. She
whispered a message, and put the little
package into cousin Harriet's hand for
Martha as she said good-by. She was very
fond of cousin Harriet. She smiled with
a gleam of her old fun; Martha's puzzled
look and tall awkward figure seemed to stand
suddenly before her eyes, as she promised
to come again to Ashford. Impatient voices
called to Helena, her lover was at the door,
and she hurried away, leaving her old home
and her girlhood gladly. If she had only
known it, as she kissed cousin Harriet good-
by, they were never going to see each other
again until they were old women. The first
step that she took out of her father's house
that day, married, and full of hope and joy,
was a step that led her away from the green
elms of Boston Common and away from her
own country and those she loved best, to
a brilliant, much-varied foreign life, and to
nearly all the sorrows and nearly all the

joys that the heart of one woman could hold
or know.

On Sunday afternoons Martha used to sit
by the window in Ashford and hold the
wooden box which a favorite young brother,
who afterward died at sea, had made for her,
and she used to take out of it the pretty little
box with a gilded cover that had held the
piece of wedding-cake, and the small scissors,
and the blurred bit of a mirror in its silver
case; as for the handkerchief with the
narrow lace edge, once in two or three years
she sprinkled it as if it were a flower, and
spread it out in the sun on the old bleaching-green, and sat near by in the shrubbery
to watch lest some bold robin or cherry-bird
should seize it and fly away.

IV.

Miss Harriet Pyne was often congrat-
ulated upon the good fortune of having such
a helper and friend as Martha.   As time
went on this tall, gaunt woman, always thin,
always slow, gained a dignity of behavior
and simple affectionateness of look which
suited the charm and dignity of the ancient
house.   She was unconsciously beautiful

like a saint, like the picturesqueness of a
lonely tree which lives to shelter unnum-
bered lives and to stand quietly in its place.
There was such rustic homeliness and con-
stancy belonging to her, such beautiful
powers of apprehension, such reticence, such
gentleness for those who were troubled or
sick; all these gifts and graces Martha hid
in her heart. She never joined the church
because she thought she was not good
enough, but life was such a passion and
happiness of service that it was impossible
not to be devout, and she was always in her
humble place on Sundays, in the back pew
next the door. She had been educated by a
remembrance; Helena's young eyes forever
looked at her reassuringly from a gay girlish
face. Helena's sweet patience in teaching
her own awkwardness could never be forgotten.

"I owe everything to Miss Helena," said
Martha, half aloud, as she sat alone by the
window; she had said it to herself a thou-
sand times. When she looked in the little
keepsake mirror she always hoped to see
some faint reflection of Helena Vernon, but
there was only her own brown old New England face to look back at her wonderingly.

Miss Pyne went less and less often to pay
visits to her friends in Boston; there were
very few friends left to come to Ashford and
make long visits in the summer, and life
grew more and more monotonous. Now and
then there came news from across the sea
and messages of remembrance, letters that
were closely written on thin sheets of paper,
and that spoke of lords and ladies, of great
journeys, of the death of little children and
the proud successes of boys at school, of the
wedding of Helena Dysart's only daughter;
but even that had happened years ago.
These things seemed far away and vague, as
if they belonged to a story and not to life
itself; the true links with the past were
quite different. There was the unvarying
flock of ground-sparrows that Helena had
begun to feed; every morning Martha scat-
tered crumbs for them from the side door-
steps while Miss Pyne watched from the
dining-room window, and they were counted
and cherished year by year.

Miss Pyne herself had many fixed habits,
but little ideality or imagination, and so at
last it was Martha who took thought for her
mistress, and gave freedom to her own good
taste. After a while, without any one's

observing the change, the every-day ways of
doing things in the house came to be the
stately ways that had once belonged only to
the entertainment of guests. Happily both
mistress and maid seized all possible chances
for hospitality, yet Miss Harriet nearly always sat alone at her exquisitely served table
with its fresh flowers, and the beautiful old
china which Martha handled so lovingly that
there was no good excuse for keeping it hidden on closet shelves. Every year when the
old cherry-trees were in fruit, Martha carried the round white old English dish with
a fretwork edge, full of pointed green leaves
and scarlet cherries, to the minister, and his
wife never quite understood why every year
he blushed and looked so conscious of the
pleasure, and thanked Martha as if he had
received a very particular attention. There
was no pretty suggestion toward the pursuit
of the fine art of housekeeping in Martha's
limited acquaintance with newspapers that
she did not adopt; there was no refined old
custom of the Pyne housekeeping that she
consented to let go. And every day, as she
had promised, she thought of Miss Helena,
— oh, many times in every day : whether
this thing would please her, or that be likely

to fall in with her fancy or ideas of fitness. As far as was possible the rare news that reached Ashford through an occasional letter or the talk of guests was made part of Martha's own life, the history of her own heart. A worn old geography often stood open at the map of Europe on the lightstand in her room, and a little old-fashioned gilt button, set with a bit of glass like a ruby, that had broken and fallen from the trimming of one of Helena's dresses, was used to mark the city of her dwelling-place. In the changes of a diplomatic life Martha followed her lady all about the map. Sometimes the button was at Paris, and sometimes at Madrid; once, to her great anxiety, it remained long at St. Petersburg. For such a slow scholar Martha was not unlearned at last, since everything about life in these foreign towns was of interest to her faithful heart. She satisfied her own mind as she threw crumbs to the tame sparrows; it was all part of the same thing and for the same affectionate reasons.

V.

One Sunday afternoon in early summer Miss Harriet Pyne came hurrying along the entry that led to Martha's room and called two or three times before its inhabitant could reach the door. Miss Harriet looked unusually cheerful and excited, and she held something in her hand. "Where are you, Martha?" she called again. "Come quick, I have something to tell you!"

"Here I am, Miss Pyne," said Martha, who had only stopped to put her precious box in the drawer, and to shut the geography.

"Who do you think is coming this very night at half-past six? We must have everything as nice as we can; I must see Hannah at once. Do you remember my cousin Helena who has lived abroad so long? Miss Helena Vernon, — the Honorable Mrs. Dysart, she is now."

"Yes, I remember her," answered Martha, turning a little pale.

"I knew that she was in this country, and I had written to ask her to come for a long visit," continued Miss Harriet, who did not often explain things, even to Martha, though she was always conscientious about the kind messages that were sent back by grateful guests. "She telegraphs that she means to anticipate her visit by a few days and come to me at once. The heat is beginning in town, I suppose. I daresay, having been a foreigner so long, she does not mind traveling on Sunday. Do you think Hannah will be prepared? We must have tea a little later."

"Yes, Miss Harriet," said Martha. She wondered that she could speak as usual, there was such a ringing in her ears. "I shall have time to pick some fresh strawberries; Miss Helena is so fond of our strawberries."

"Why, I had forgotten," said Miss Pyne, a little puzzled by something quite unusual in Martha's face. "We must expect to find Mrs. Dysart a good deal changed, Martha; it is a great many years since she was here; I have not seen her since her wedding, and she has had a great deal of trouble, poor girl. You had better open the parlor chamber, and make it ready before you go down."

"It is all ready," said Martha. "I can carry some of those little sweet-brier roses upstairs before she comes."

"Yes, you are always thoughtful," said Miss Pyne, with unwonted feeling.

Martha did not answer. She glanced at the telegram wistfully. She had never really suspected before that Miss Pyne knew nothing of the love that had been in her heart all these years; it was half a pain and half a golden joy to keep such a secret; she could hardly bear this moment of surprise.

Presently the news gave wings to her willing feet. When Hannah, the cook, who never had known Miss Helena, went to the parlor an hour later on some errand to her old mistress, she discovered that this stranger guest must be a very important person. She had never seen the tea-table look exactly as it did that night, and in the parlor itself there were fresh blossoming boughs in the old East India jars, and lilies in the paneled hall, and flowers everywhere, as if there were some high festivity.

Miss Pyne sat by the window watching, in her best dress, looking stately and calm; she seldom went out now, and it was almost time for the carriage. Martha was just coming in from the garden with the strawberries, and with more flowers in her apron. It was a bright cool evening in June, the golden robins sang in the elms, and the sun was going down behind the apple-trees at the foot of the garden. The beautiful old house stood wide open to the long-expected guest.

"I think that I shall go down to the gate," said Miss Pyne, looking at Martha for approval, and Martha nodded and they went together slowly down the broad front walk.

There was a sound of horses and wheels on the roadside turf: Martha could not see at first; she stood back inside the gate behind the white lilac-bushes as the carriage came. Miss Pyne was there; she was holding out both arms and taking a tired, bent little figure in black to her heart. "Oh, my Miss Helena is an old woman like me!" and Martha gave a pitiful sob; she had never dreamed it would be like this; this was the one thing she could not bear.

"Where are you, Martha?" called Miss Pyne. "Martha will bring these in; you have not forgotten my good Martha, Helena?" Then Mrs. Dysart looked up and smiled just as she used to smile in the old days. The young eyes were there still in the changed face, and Miss Helena had come.

That night Martha waited in her lady's room just as she used, humble and silent, and went through with the old unforgotten loving services. The long years seemed like days. At last she lingered a moment trying to think of something else that might be done, then she was going silently away, but Helena called her back. She suddenly knew the whole story and could hardly speak.

" Oh, my dear Martha ! " she cried, " won't you kiss me good-night ? Oh, Martha, have you remembered like this, all these long years ! "

This is the end of this publication.

Any remaining blank pages are for our book binding requirements and are blank on purpose.

To search thousands of interesting publications like this one, please remember to visit our website at:

http://www.kessinger.net

CPSIA information can be obtained at www.ICGtesting.com
Printed in the USA
LVOW04s2108230914

405481LV00027B/927/P